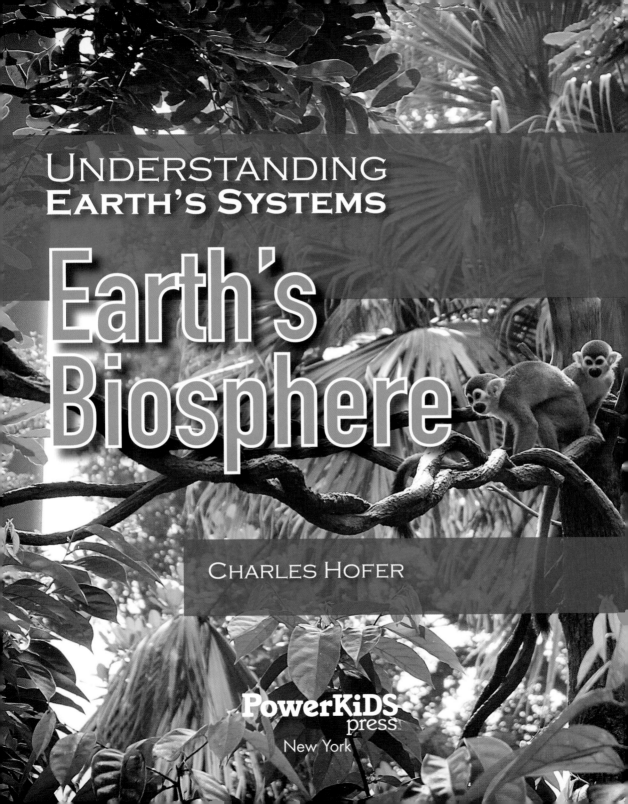

# UNDERSTANDING EARTH'S SYSTEMS

# Earth's Biosphere

## CHARLES HOFER

**PowerKiDS** press

New York

Published in 2019 by The Rosen Publishing Group, Inc.
29 East 21st Street, New York, NY 10010

First Edition

Editor: Elizabeth Krajnik
Book Design: Rachel Rising

Photo Credits: Cover, p.1 LittleLulu/Shutterstock.com; pp. 3, 4, 6, 8 ,10, 12, 14, 16, 18, 20, 22, 24, 26, 28, 30, 31, 32 (background) Maxim Tupikov/Shutterstock.com; p. 4 Chinnapong/Shutterstock.com; p. 5 MarcelClemens/Shutterstock.com; p. 7 Darkydoors/Shutterstock.com; p. 8 Hannamariah/Shutterstock.com; pp. 9, 11, 13, 25, 27 (background) Stacy Barnett/Shutterstock.com; p. 9 Designua/Shutterstock.com; p. 11 (grass and dandelions) Sergej Razvodovskij/Shutterstock.com; p. 11 (fox, rabbit) Felix Broennimann/Shutterstock.com; p. 13 SCIENCE SOURCE/Science Source/Getty Images; p. 15 (forest) Guenter Albers/Shutterstock.com; p. 15 (desert) Dmitry Pichugin/Shutterstock.com; p. 15 (tundra) Honza Krej/Shutterstock.com; p. 15 (grassland) Paul Hampton/Shutterstock.com; p. 15 (aquatic) Martin 175/Shutterstock.com; p. 17 (tropical forest) Quick Shot/Shutterstock.com; p. 17 (temperate forest) effective stock photos/Shutterstock.com; p. 19 Jim David/Shutterstock.com; p. 20 koya979/Shutterstock.com; p. 21 Karelian/Shutterstock.com; p. 23 Lotus_studio/Shutterstock.com; p. 25 Avanta/Shutterstock.com; p. 26 Potapov Alexander/Shutterstock.com; p. 27 2630ben/Shutterstock.com; p. 29 irabel8/Shutterstock.com; p. 30 stockyimages/Shutterstock.com.

Cataloging-in-Publication Data

Names: Hofer, Charles.
Title: Earth's biosphere / Charles Hofer.
Description: New York : PowerKids Press, 2019. | Series: Understanding Earth's systems | Includes glossary and index.
Identifiers: ISBN 9781538329856 (pbk.) | ISBN 9781538329832 (library bound) | ISBN 9781538329863 (6 pack)
Subjects: LCSH: Earth (Planet)–Juvenile literature. | Biosphere–Juvenile literature. | Biotic communities–Juvenile literature.
Classification: LCC QB631.4 H65 2019 | DDC 525–dc23

Manufactured in the United States of America

CPSIA Compliance Information: Batch #CS18PK: For Further Information contact Rosen Publishing, New York, New York at 1-800-237-9932

# Contents

# Our Living Planet

Earth is a special planet in our solar system. It's the only planet known to support life. Pictures of Earth from space show its swirling cloud patterns, bright white poles, blue-black oceans, and sandy deserts.

Everything on Earth—including Earth itself—can be placed into one of four **spheres**, or the systems in which Earth's many processes occur. While each sphere is **unique**, they work together to keep Earth functioning normally.

The atmosphere is the whole mass of air that surrounds Earth. The geosphere is the solid earth and all Earth's layers. The hydrosphere is the water on Earth, in all its forms.

The biosphere is the part of Earth in which life can exist. Within the biosphere, living creatures—from tiny single-celled organisms to huge mammals—constantly interact with their **environments** in a never-ending cycle of life and death.

The geosphere, hydrosphere, atmosphere, and biosphere constantly interact to make life on Earth possible.

# In the Beginning

Earth is about 4.5 billion years old. Scientists estimate that life appeared on Earth about 3.7 billion years ago. These life-forms were microbes, or extremely small living things that can only be seen with a microscope. From these life-forms stemmed other life-forms, such as bacteria, dinosaurs, and human beings.

In Greenland, there are fossils of cyanobacteria, or blue-green algae, that are older than 3.7 billion years old. These fossils are called stromatolites and are one of the earliest signs of life existing on Earth. However, these might not be the first life-forms on Earth. Some scientists think that because these organisms are so complex, life must have started well before 3.7 billion years ago.

Even though scientists have a large amount of information about when life on Earth may have first appeared, they aren't exactly sure what processes took place to make life possible.

These stromatolites were found in Hamelin Pool Marine Nature Reserve in Western Australia.

## SYSTEM CONNECTIONS

*Bio* is the Greek word for "life." This means that "biosphere" is the sphere of life and "biology" is the study of life.

# It's Alive!

Earth's four spheres interact through processes that are both biotic, or living, and abiotic, or nonliving. These processes keep food and energy in motion. Just as the water cycle takes place mainly in the hydrosphere and atmosphere, the biosphere features a number of unique processes. The oxygen cycle, the nitrogen cycle, and other cycles constantly move life-giving **elements** through the biosphere.

The changing of seasons, weather, and climate are examples of abiotic processes that affect the biosphere. Weather is the state of the air and atmosphere at a particular time and place. Climate is the average weather conditions of a place over a period of years. These abiotic factors constantly influence the biosphere's **biota**, creating a **dynamic** biosphere.

When humans burn **fossil fuels,** carbon dioxide is released into the atmosphere. Carbon dioxide is also released into the atmosphere when animals breathe.

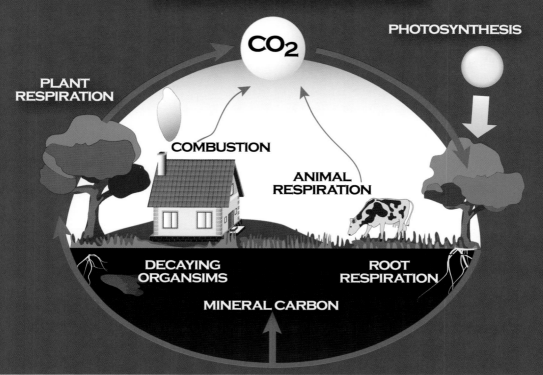

## THE CARBON CYCLE

PHOTOSYNTHESIS

CO₂

PLANT RESPIRATION

COMBUSTION

ANIMAL RESPIRATION

DECAYING ORGANSIMS

ROOT RESPIRATION

MINERAL CARBON

# The Carbon Cycle

Carbon is often described as "the building block of life." Every living thing—and many nonliving things—is made up of carbon. This life-giving element is constantly moving within the biosphere through the carbon cycle. Most plants grow by absorbing, or taking in, carbon dioxide from Earth's atmosphere. Animals—such as humans—take in carbon by eating plants or other animals. When plants and animals die, carbon dioxide is returned to the biosphere to keep the cycle in motion.

# The Giver of Life

The sun provides energy for all life on Earth. It does this through photosynthesis, the process by which green plants and a few other organisms turn water and carbon dioxide into food in the presence of sunlight.

Everything in the biosphere fits into at least one food chain, which is comprised of producers, consumers, and decomposers. Producers, also known as autotrophs, make their own food through photosynthesis. The only organisms that do this are plants, algae, phytoplankton, and bacteria. Producers are the first organisms on all food chains.

Primary consumers called herbivores get their energy from consuming producers. Secondary consumers get their energy from consuming the primary consumer and producers. Tertiary consumers get their energy from eating the secondary consumers. Decomposers get their energy from decomposing, or breaking down, dead plant and animal matter.

The farther down an organism is in a food chain, the more **biomass** it must consume to stay alive. There are always fewer organisms at the end of a food chain than at the beginning.

## A GREAT PLAINS FOOD CHAIN

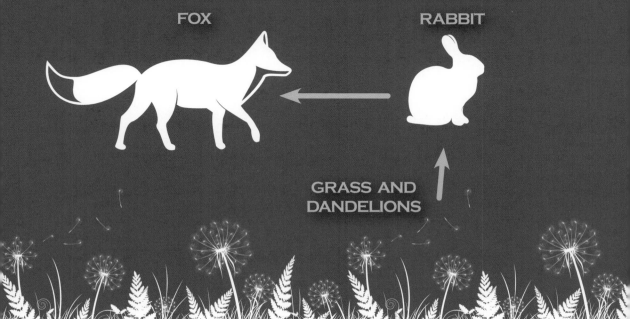

FOX

RABBIT

GRASS AND DANDELIONS

# Trophic Levels and Energy Pyramids

Food chains are broken down into trophic levels. Autotrophs are the first level, herbivores are the second level, and carnivores and omnivores are the third level. When a number of food chains interact, they form a food web. Energy pyramids describe how energy is lost from one trophic level to the next. As organisms are consumed, only about 10 percent of the energy from that organism is transferred, or given over to, the organism at the next level.

# Evolution by Natural Selection

All **species** of plants and animals must **adapt** to fit their environment. If they don't, they'll go extinct, or die out. This process is called natural selection or "survival of the fittest." Organisms that are better adapted to their environment are the ones that reproduce successfully. Then they pass on the desired **traits** to their offspring. The organisms that are less fit for their environment do not reproduce as quickly as other species, and eventually die out.

For example, white mice are easier for predators to see on the dark forest floor. Therefore, the white mice are eaten by hawks first. If there are no white mice left to reproduce, the trait for white fur won't be passed on to the next generation.

**Evolution** by natural selection has created some amazing animal and plant adaptations. Natural selection can also cause species to behave a certain way. An example of this would be an animal's mating ritual.

Darwin observed natural selection in the beaks of finches on the Galápagos Islands. After droughts in 2003, scientists noted the finches' beaks became deeper and stronger, allowing them to eat tougher seeds.

# Darwin's Evolution

English naturalist Charles Darwin shook the world when he published his theories on evolution in 1859. In his book, *On the Origin of Species*, Darwin explained how species can change over time through natural selection. Darwin developed his remarkable theories by studying life on islands, like the Galápagos Islands off the coast of Ecuador. To Darwin, islands were living laboratories where evolution could be seen in real time.

# Biomes

We can separate Earth's surface into different communities based on climate, types of soil, and the species of plants and animals that live there. These communities are called biomes. There are five major biomes: forest, desert, tundra, grassland, and aquatic.

Each biome can be further separated into smaller ecosystems that are more specialized. Ecosystems are the interaction of living and nonliving things in an environment. A good example of the difference between a biome and an ecosystem is that in the forest biome you can find a number of ecosystems, such as a canopy ecosystem and an understory ecosystem in a tropical forest biome.

Biomes change over time. For example, the Sahara Desert wasn't always as large as it is today. Parts of it used to be lush and green. However, the climate changed and the lush, green areas dried out and became covered with sand.

FOREST

DESERT

TUNDRA

GRASSLAND

AQUATIC

# Tropical and Temperate Forests

Tropical forests are home to many different plant and animal species. These forests occur near the equator and are known for having only two seasons—rainy and dry. The temperature remains fairly constant—usually 68 to 77°F (20 to 25°C)—throughout the year and these areas receive more than 78 inches (2,000 mm) of rain annually. Lush canopies prevent light from reaching the forest floor. Many different plant species—more than 100 species of trees alone—call tropical forests home. Some trees reach 114 feet (35 m) tall!

Temperate forests, which exist in eastern North America, northeastern Asia, and western and central Europe, experience all seasons. The temperature varies greatly, between −22 and 86°F (−30 and 30°C). Temperate forests receive far less precipitation than tropical forests, and the canopies there allow light to reach the forest floor.

In tropical forests, the growing seasons are long with periods of heavy rainfall. In temperate forests, however, plants and animals have adapted to long, cold winters.

# SYSTEM CONNECTIONS

Soil in tropical forests is loose and lacks **nutrients** due to heavy rains. The process of soil losing nutrients due to heavy rain is called leaching.

# Deserts and Grasslands

Deserts biomes are characterized by receiving less than 20 inches (51 cm) of rainfall per year. Deserts have few species of plants and animals, which are highly adapted to living there. Soil in deserts is usually nutrient rich. Deserts experience wildfires, cold weather, and flash floods. There are different types of deserts, including hot and dry (such as the Sahara Desert), semiarid (such as the Australian outback), coastal (such as the Atacama Desert), and cold (such as the entire continent of Antarctica).

Grassland biomes are large areas covered mostly by grasses rather than trees. Grasslands are divided into two types: tropical grasslands called savannas and temperate grasslands. Here, grasses and many other plants are drought tolerant, meaning they can go long periods without rain. Grasslands are home to large, migrating, herd animals, such as elephants in Africa and pronghorns in North America.

Grassland soils can be stripped of nutrients if the same crops are grown on the same land year after year. When the soil lacks nutrients, crops can't be grown there for a number of years.

# SYSTEM CONNECTIONS

Many grasslands have been turned into farmland due to their nutrient-rich soil. As a consequence, many grassland species have been wiped out. These areas often experience drought, which further puts their plant and animal life in danger.

# Tundra and Taiga

The tundra biome is characterized by having few trees, very low temperatures, little precipitation, and **permafrost**. The two types of tundra are arctic tundra and alpine tundra. The arctic tundra circles the North Pole and reaches down to the taiga. Its growing season is very short at just 50 to 60 days. The plants of the arctic tundra are adapted to resisting strong winds and cold temperatures. The alpine tundra exists on mountains around the world at elevations above which trees can't grow. The growing season is about 180 days and the soil there drains well, unlike that of the arctic tundra.

The taiga, or boreal forests, is the largest land biome. This biome exists just south of the arctic tundra and is characterized by short, wet, and somewhat warm summers and long, cold, and dry winters. The growing season in the taiga is only 130 days.

Tundra biomes are known for having cycles in population sizes. For example, if the population of lemmings grows too large, groups of lemmings will migrate to find less crowded places to live.

# SYSTEM CONNECTIONS

Loggers often remove trees from taiga regions. Logging practices may cause certain species of plants and animals to go extinct due to habitat loss.

# Marine and Freshwater Biomes

The aquatic biome is any part of Earth covered with water, which can be broken down into freshwater regions and marine regions. Ponds, lakes, rivers, streams, and freshwater wetlands are part of freshwater regions. Freshwater regions have a salt concentration of less than 1 percent, and the plants and animals that survive there can't survive in marine regions.

The marine region is made up of Earth's oceans, coral reefs, and estuaries. These regions cover more than three-fourths of Earth's surface. The largest parts of the marine region are the oceans, which can be separated into zones based on depth and the species living there.

Most marine life occurs near the surface of the ocean where sunlight can penetrate. This area is called the photic zone. Here, tiny organisms called phytoplankton make their own food through photosynthesis and are the base of the giant marine food web.

Coral reefs are often called the "rainforests of the oceans" because they are home to most of Earth's marine species.

# SYSTEM CONNECTIONS

Deep-ocean ecosystems are dark, and some organisms have evolved to produce their own light through chemical reactions. This is known as bioluminescence.

# Human Beings

Many of Earth's life-forms have been around for billions of years. However, human beings have been around for only 1.8 million years or so. These early humans, called *Homo erectus*, are the earliest creatures showing similarities to present-day humans, or *Homo sapiens*. Humans are primates, and the closest relation we have are gorillas, chimpanzees, and bonobos. Together, we all fit into the great ape family, Hominidae.

*Homo sapiens* evolved in Africa around 200,000 years ago. These humans, like other species before them, were hunters and gatherers. They evolved to adapt to their surroundings. They used specialized tools to help them deal with their environments and hunt. The brains of *Homo sapiens* are much larger than our ancestors' brains, allowing us to interact with each other. As a result, humans have been able to move to the far reaches of Earth and grow in number. There are now 7.6 billion of us.

Earth's population is the largest it's ever been. The biosphere has to support all humans and all living things. To ensure Earth continues to support us, it's necessary to do things to take care of it, such as recycling and planting trees.

# Ecosystem Services

Ecosystem services are the benefits that humans get from a healthy biosphere. They can be broken down into four categories: provisioning, regulating, habitat, and cultural services. Provisioning services are products from ecosystems to keep life going, such as food and medicine. Regulating services are when Earth works to keep ecosystems going through processes such as water purification and pollination. Habitat services are when ecosystems provide habitats to ensure the passage of traits through offspring. Cultural services include ways humans enjoy ecosystems, such as by participating in outdoor sports or admiring nature-themed art.

# Biodiversity

Preserving Earth's **biodiversity** is more important than ever. Every organism in the biosphere plays an important role in its ecosystem. This biodiversity creates a stable and healthy biosphere. When we lose biodiversity, however, we risk upsetting the delicate balance that keeps the ecosystems within our biosphere functioning properly.

Many scientists believe we are experiencing another great extinction, the likes of which Earth hasn't seen since the dinosaurs vanished about 65 million years ago. Today, Earth is losing species—losing biodiversity—at an alarming rate. All of the food on Earth comes directly from the plants and animals within the biosphere. More than 75 percent of our medicines come from the biosphere too. Extinction is permanent. We must be careful that we aren't treating the biosphere wastefully, and do our best to replace what we take from it.

*Diceros bocornis longipes,* commonly known as the western black rhinoceros, has been extinct since 2011. These creatures were killed for their horns.

# The Importance of Bees

We can find bees anywhere flowers bloom. In the United States alone, there are 4,000 native bee species. Native bee species do most of the pollination, not honeybees. Pollination is an ecosystem service. Bees pollinate about 80 percent of flowering plants. Some species of native bees and honeybees are experiencing population declines. It's important we work to prevent bees from going extinct. Without bees to pollinate plants, about 75 percent of the fruits, nuts, and vegetables grown in the United States would likely die out.

# Climate Change

Earth's climate is changing. Driven mainly by humans' overuse of fossil fuels, global average temperatures are expected to rise 3.6°F (2°C) by the year 2100. As a result, the polar ice caps are melting and oceans are warming, leading to more frequent and powerful storms. Earth is becoming drier in many locations, deserts are expanding, and stores of fresh water are dropping to critical levels. Plants and animals all over the world will have to adapt or risk going extinct.

Unfortunately, humans are no longer the exception to these rules of adaptation. We will need to find new ways to protect and manage our natural resources—the nutrient-rich soil, plentiful fresh water, plants, and animals we need for our biosphere to function properly. Then, we may be able to adapt to our rapidly changing world.

Large-scale desalination plants can change undrinkable salt water into fresh water for human use. However, these plants are expensive to build and require lots of energy to run.

# SYSTEM CONNECTIONS

Habitat loss is one of the greatest threats to Earth's biodiversity. When we cut down forests or build cities, we destroy the habitats in which plants and animals live.

# The Biosphere Feeds Us

We need our biosphere and our biosphere needs us. Each biome plays an important role in the overall health of the planet. We need to protect the species and their ecosystems. When we lose biodiversity, we lose more than just one animal or plant. We might also lose some or all of the animals that depend on that animal for survival. Or we may lose an important ingredient in a life-saving medicine. If we aren't careful, our biosphere could one day collapse.

All of the resources that support life are in the biosphere right now. We don't have the ability to add any more than what's already there. However, we do have the ability to protect these resources and use them wisely. We can't get back the species that have already gone extinct, but we can prevent other species from dying out from human activities.

# Glossary

**adapt:** To change in order to live better in a certain environment.

**biodiversity:** The existence of many different kinds of plants and animals in an environment.

**biomass:** The amount of living matter in a habitat.

**biota:** The plants and animals of a region.

**dynamic:** Always active or changing.

**element:** Matter that's pure and has no other type of matter in it.

**environment:** The conditions that surround a living thing and affect the way it lives.

**evolution:** The process of change in an animal or a plant species over long periods of time.

**fossil fuel:** A fuel—such as coal, oil, or natural gas—that is formed in the earth from dead plants or animals.

**nutrient:** Something taken in by a plant or animal that helps it grow and stay healthy.

**permafrost:** A layer of soil that is always frozen.

**species:** A group of plants or animals that are all the same kind.

**sphere:** An area of activity, existence, or authority. It also means an object shaped like a ball.

**trait:** A quality that makes one person or thing different from another.

**unique:** Special or different from anything else.

# Index

# Websites

Due to the changing nature of Internet links, PowerKids Press has developed an online list of websites related to the subject of this book. This site is updated regularly. Please use this link to access the list: www.powerkidslinks.com/ues/bio